Elements 1 - 18

The 7 pieces for Module A are on this page and pages 3 ...

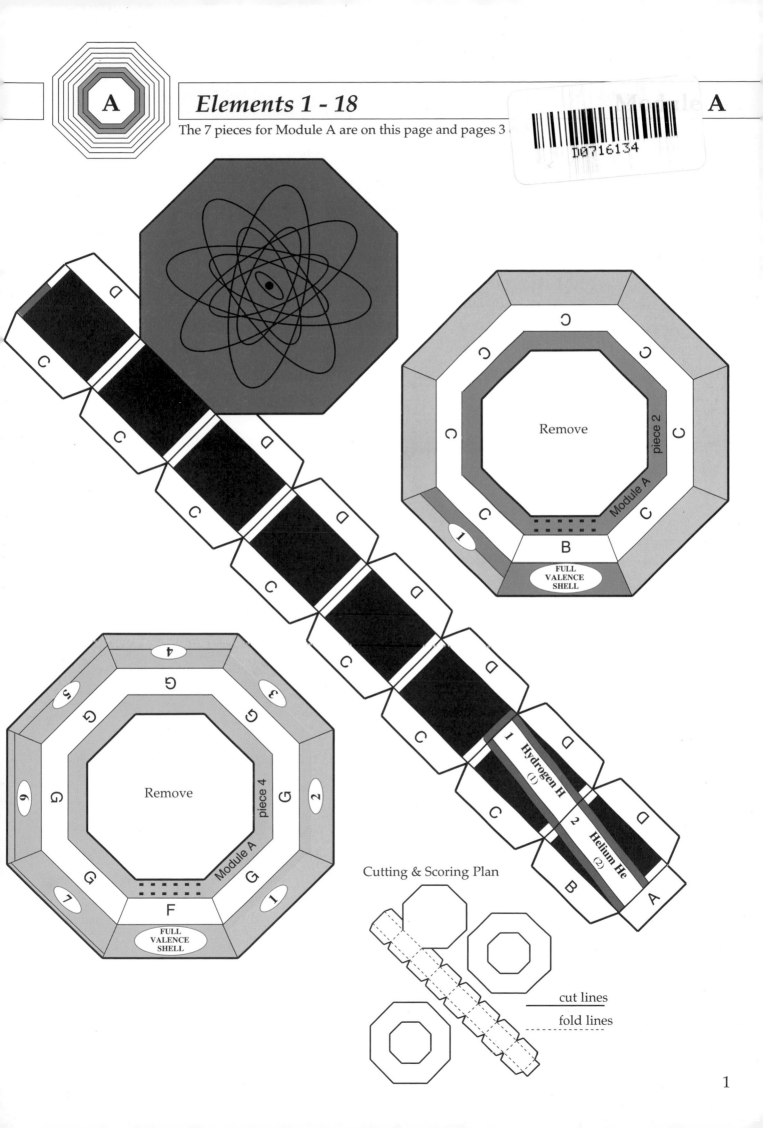

Remove

Module A

piece 2

B

FULL
VALENCE
SHELL

C

Hydrogen H
(1)

Helium He
(2)

Remove

Module A

piece 4

F

FULL
VALENCE
SHELL

Cutting & Scoring Plan

cut lines

fold lines

1

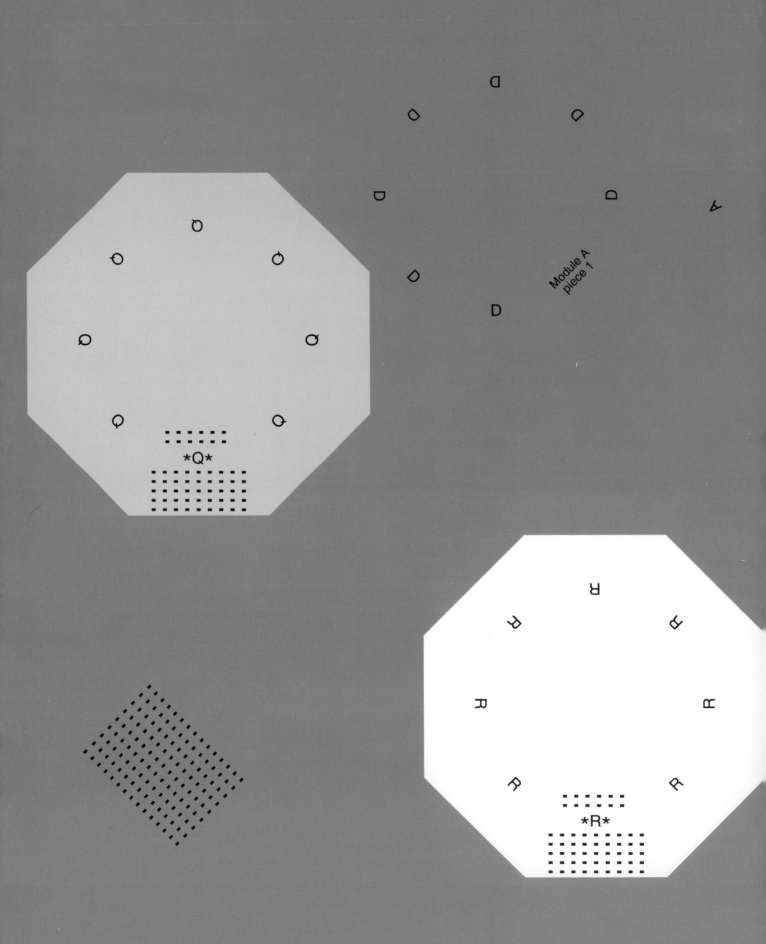

Module A
piece 1

Q

R

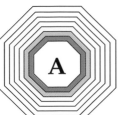

The 7 pieces for Module A are on this page and pages 1 & 5.

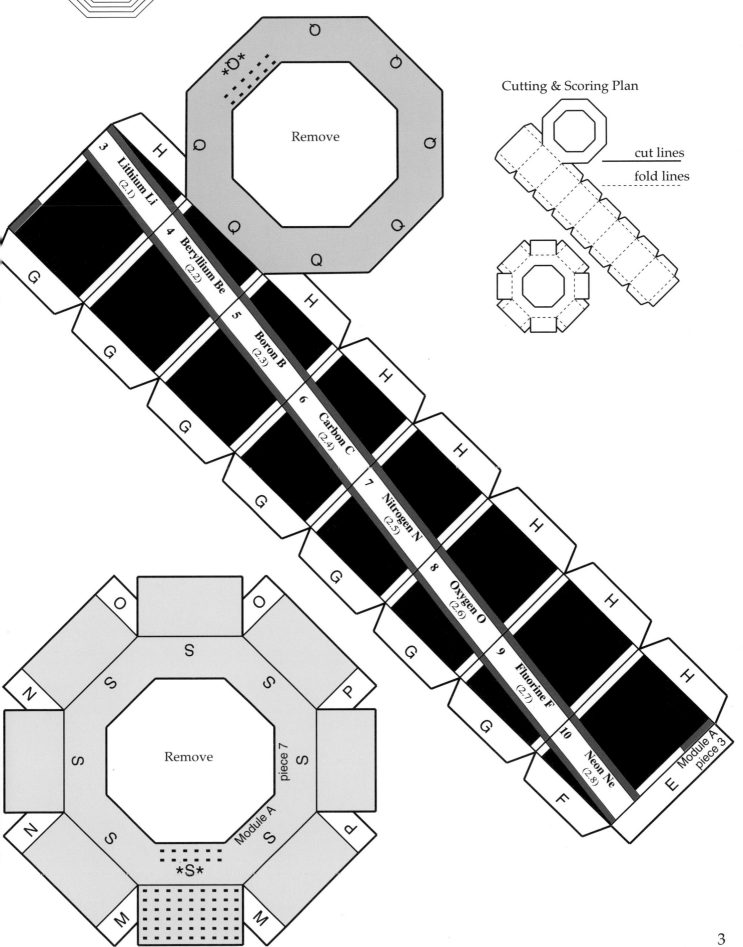

Cutting & Scoring Plan

cut lines

fold lines

Remove

Q Q *Q* Q Q Q Q Q

3 H

Lithium Li (2.1)

4 Beryllium Be (2.2)

5 Boron B (2.3)

6 Carbon C (2.4)

7 Nitrogen N (2.5)

8 Oxygen O (2.6)

9 Fluorine F (2.7)

10 Neon Ne (2.8)

G G G G G G G G

H H H H H H H

Module A piece 3

E

F

O O S S S S N N S S S P P

Remove

piece 7 Module A

S M M

H

H

H

H

H

E

H

H

O   O

d

N

P

N

M   M

The 7 pieces for Module A are on this page and pages 1 & 3.

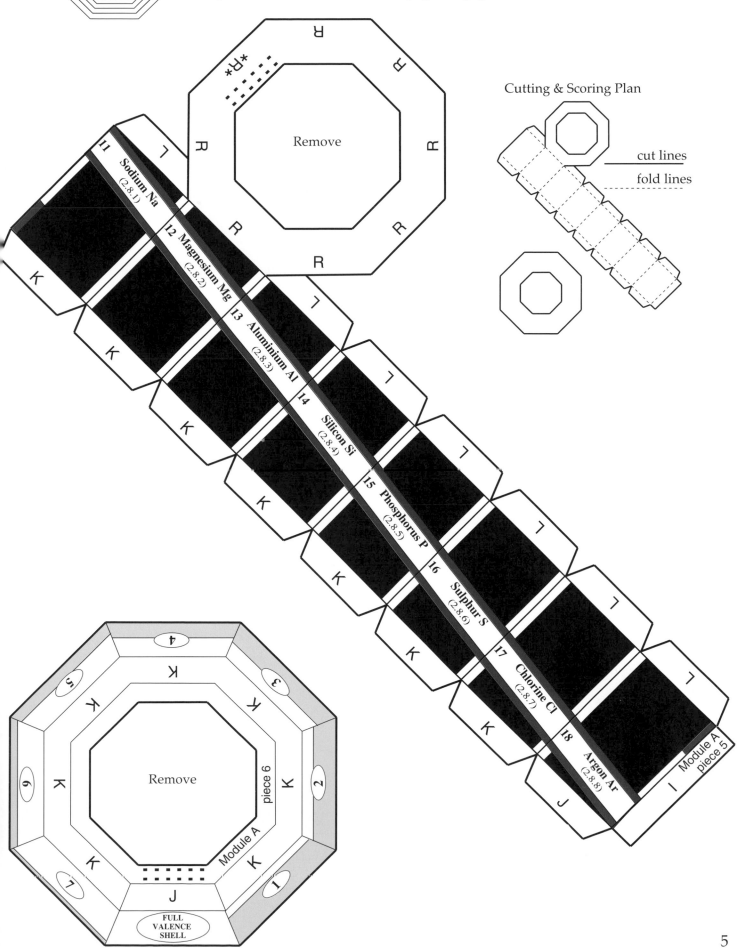

Remove

Cutting & Scoring Plan

cut lines

fold lines

11 **Sodium Na** (2.8.1)

12 **Magnesium Mg** (2.8.2)

13 **Aluminium Al** (2.8.3)

14 **Silicon Si** (2.8.4)

15 **Phosphorus P** (2.8.5)

16 **Sulphur S** (2.8.6)

17 **Chlorine Cl** (2.8.7)

18 **Argon Ar** (2.8.8)

Module A piece 5

Remove

piece 6

Module A

FULL VALENCE SHELL

S

The 6 pieces for Module B are on this page and pages 9 & 23.

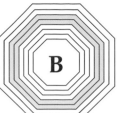

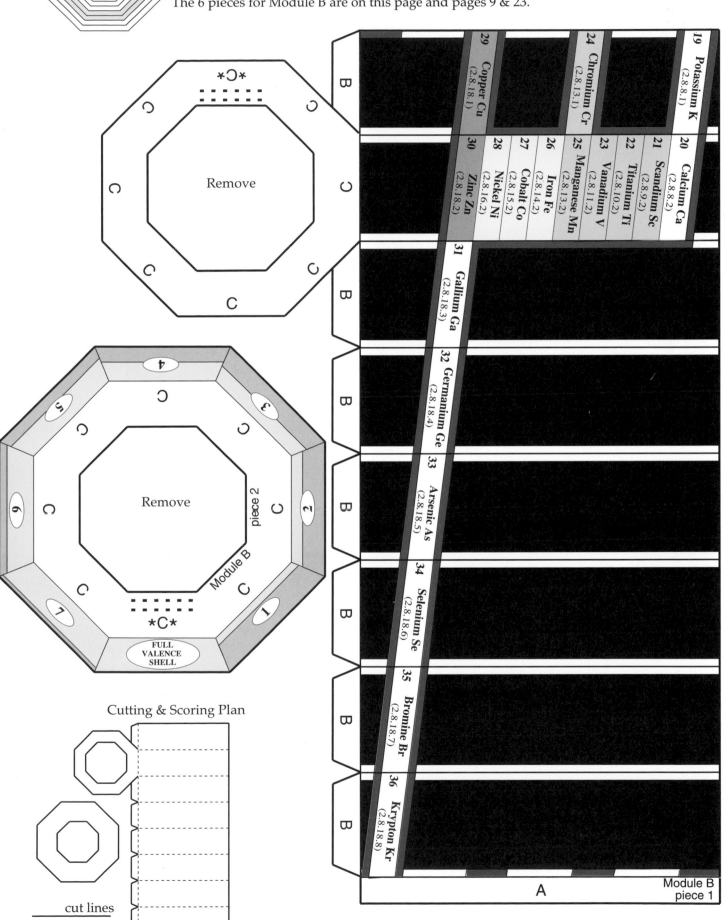

Remove

C

Remove

Module B
piece 2

FULL
VALENCE
SHELL

Cutting & Scoring Plan

cut lines
fold lines

19	Potassium K (2.8.8.1)
20	Calcium Ca (2.8.8.2)
21	Scandium Sc (2.8.9.2)
22	Titanium Ti (2.8.10.2)
23	Vanadium V (2.8.11.2)
24	Chromium Cr (2.8.13.1)
25	Manganese Mn (2.8.13.2)
26	Iron Fe (2.8.14.2)
27	Cobalt Co (2.8.15.2)
28	Nickel Ni (2.8.16.2)
29	Copper Cu (2.8.18.1)
30	Zinc Zn (2.8.18.2)
31	Gallium Ga (2.8.18.3)
32	Germanium Ge (2.8.18.4)
33	Arsenic As (2.8.18.5)
34	Selenium Se (2.8.18.6)
35	Bromine Br (2.8.18.7)
36	Krypton Kr (2.8.18.8)

A

Module B
piece 1

A

B

B   B   B

B

B   B

B

M

M   M

M   M

M   M

```
: : : : : :
```
M
```
■ ■ ■ ■ ■ ■ ■
■ ■ ■ ■ ■ ■ ■
■ ■ ■ ■ ■ ■ ■
■ ■ ■ ■ ■ ■ ■
```

```
■ ■ ■ ■ ■ ■ ■ ■ ■ ■ ■ ■ ■ ■ ■ ■ ■ ■ ■ ■ ■ ■ ■ ■ ■ ■
■ ■ ■ ■ ■ ■ ■ ■ ■ ■ ■ ■ ■ ■ ■ ■ ■ ■ ■ ■ ■ ■ ■ ■ ■ ■
■ ■ ■ ■ ■ ■ ■ ■ ■ ■ ■ ■ ■ ■ ■ ■ ■ ■ ■ ■ ■ ■ ■ ■ ■ ■
■ ■ ■ ■ ■ ■ ■ ■ ■ ■ ■ ■ ■ ■ ■ ■ ■ ■ ■ ■ ■ ■ ■ ■ ■ ■
■ ■ ■ ■ ■ ■ ■ ■ ■ ■ ■ ■ ■ ■ ■ ■ ■ ■ ■ ■ ■ ■ ■ ■ ■ ■
■ ■ ■ ■ ■ ■ ■ ■ ■ ■ ■ ■ ■ ■ ■ ■ ■ ■ ■ ■ ■ ■ ■ ■ ■ ■
```

The 6 pieces for Module B are on this page and pages 7 & 23.

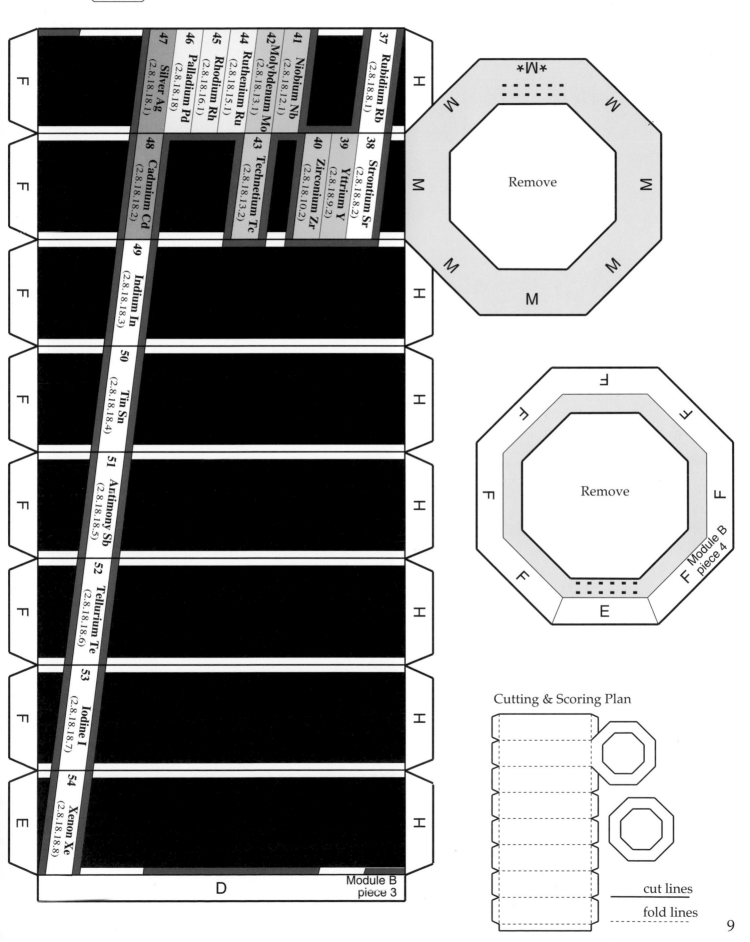

37 Rubidium Rb (2.8.18.8.1)

41 Niobium Nb (2.8.18.12.1)

42 Molybdenum Mo (2.8.18.13.1)

44 Ruthenium Ru (2.8.18.15.1)

45 Rhodium Rh (2.8.18.16.1)

46 Palladium Pd (2.8.18.18)

47 Silver Ag (2.8.18.18.1)

38 Strontium Sr (2.8.18.8.2)

39 Yttrium Y (2.8.18.9.2)

40 Zirconium Zr (2.8.18.10.2)

43 Technetium Tc (2.8.18.13.2)

48 Cadmium Cd (2.8.18.18.2)

49 Indium In (2.8.18.18.3)

50 Tin Sn (2.8.18.18.4)

51 Antimony Sb (2.8.18.18.5)

52 Tellurium Te (2.8.18.18.6)

53 Iodine I (2.8.18.18.7)

54 Xenon Xe (2.8.18.18.8)

Module B piece 3

M
Remove

F
Remove
Module B piece 4
E

Cutting & Scoring Plan

cut lines

fold lines

9

D

H

H

H

H

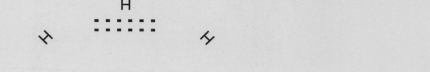

H

H

H

G

G

G

G

G

G

G

G

The Anatomy of the Atom

&

the structure of the periodic table

Gerald Jenkins
Magdalen Bear

The Discovery of the Elements

Known in Ancient Times
- 6 Carbon
- 16 Sulphur
- 26 Iron
- 29 Copper
- 47 Silver
- 50 Tin
- 79 Gold
- 80 Mercury
- 82 Lead

c1250 33 Arsenic
c1450 51 Antimony
c1450 83 Bismuth
c1500 30 Zinc
c1500 78 Platinum

1669 15 Phosphorus
1735 27 Cobalt
1751 28 Nickel
1766 1 Hydrogen
1771 9 Fluorine
1772 7 Nitrogen
1774 8 Oxygen
- 17 Chlorine
- 25 Manganese
1775 12 Magnesium
1778 42 Molybdenum
1782 52 Tellurium
1783 74 Tungsten
1789 40 Zirconium
1790 38 Strontium
1791 22 Titanium
1794 39 Yttrium
1797 24 Chromium
1801 41 Niobium
1802 73 Tantalum
1803 45 Rhodium
- 46 Palladium
- 58 Cerium

1804 76 Osmium
- 77 Iridium
1807 11 Sodium
- 19 Potassium
1808 5 Boron
- 20 Calcium
- 56 Barium
1811 53 Iodine
1817 3 Lithium
- 34 Selenium
- 48 Cadmium
1823 14 Silicon
1826 35 Bromine
1827 13 Aluminium
1828 4 Beryllium
- 90 Thorium
1839 57 Lanthanum
1841 92 Uranium
1843 65 Terbium
- 68 Erbium
1844 44 Ruthenium
1860 55 Caesium
1861 37 Rubidium
- 81 Thallium
1863 49 Indium
1867 23 Vanadium
1868 2 Helium
1875 31 Gallium
1879 21 Scandium
- 62 Samarium
- 67 Holmium
- 69 Thulium
1880 64 Gadolinium
1885 59 Praseodymium
- 60 Neodymium
1886 32 Germanium
- 66 Dysprosium
1894 18 Argon
1896 63 Europium

1898 10 Neon
- 36 Krypton
- 54 Xenon
- 84 Polonium
- 88 Radium
1899 89 Actinium
1900 86 Radon
1907 70 Ytterbium
- 71 Lutetium
1917 91 Protactinium
1923 72 Hafnium
1925 75 Rhenium
1937 43 Technetium
1939 87 Francium
1940 85 Astatine
- 93 Neptunium
- 94 Plutonium
1944 95 Americium
- 96 Curium
1947 61 Promethium
1949 97 Berkelium
1950 98 Californium
1952 99 Einsteinium
- 100 Fermium
1955 101 Mendelevium
1958 102 Nobelium
1961 103 Lawrencium

Since 1980
- 104 Rutherfordium
- 105 Dubnium
- 106 Seaborgium
- 107 Bohrium
- 108 Hassium
- 109 Meitnerium
- 110 Ununnilium
- 111 Unununium
- 112 Ununbium

Tarquin

0 906212 97 9

2

A Remarkable Discovery

The 'Chemical Helix' model is a celebration of one of the greatest achievements of science, the discovery of the electronic structure of the atom. We are now in the fortunate position of being able to make use of this knowledge to explain and understand many things which were a mystery and a puzzle to our ancestors.

This achievement is not the work of a single individual or even of a small group of people, nor is it confined to one country or one period of time. It is truly international and is the culmination of the work of countless thousands of researchers over a very long period.

Throughout history, chemical research has been driven by two different desires. The first was the practical need to make and develop useful substances and the second, the intellectual drive to understand the fundamentals of the universe. There has not generally been too much conflict between these two motives because the better the understanding of fundamentals, the easier it becomes to develop useful new materials.

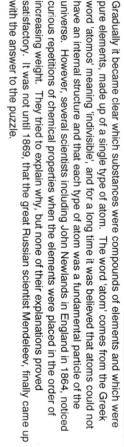

Gradually it became clear which substances were compounds of elements and which were pure elements, made up of a single type of atom. The word 'atom' comes from the Greek word 'atomos' meaning 'indivisible', and for a long time it was believed that atoms could not have an internal structure and that each type of atom was a fundamental particle of the universe. However, several scientists including John Newlands in England in 1864, noticed curious repetitions of chemical properties when the elements were placed in the order of increasing weight. They tried to explain why, but none of their explanations proved satisfactory. It was not until 1869, that the great Russian scientist Mendeleev, finally came up with the answer to the puzzle.

At the time, some 63 different elements were known and Mendeleev had filled in a separate card for each. On each card he wrote down the chemical properties and other information known about that element. He then tried to sort the cards into a sensible order, asking himself in particular which element should come first. Perhaps it should be oxygen because it was essential for life? Perhaps it should be gold because it was so valuable? Perhaps it should be oxygen because it was essential for life? Perhaps hydrogen because it was the lightest? He noticed that the atomic weights of many elements were approximately a whole number of times greater than that of hydrogen and decided to arrange his cards in order of increasing atomic weight. He gave each element a reference number (the atomic number) based on its position in this list and then noticed that if he placed the cards into seven columns, elements with similar chemical and physical properties came above and beneath each other in the table. Why seven columns? He did not know, but so strongly did he believe in his idea that he had the courage to leave gaps and to say that they would be filled by elements yet to be discovered. He even forecast the properties these new elements would have.

It is hard for us nowadays to appreciate what a great step it was. It is impossible for us not to know that atoms do have an internal structure and are made from protons, neutrons and electrons. We may even be aware that there are other particles too. However, his work is the work of genius and his discovery was **The Periodic Table**. The chemical helix model is a three-dimensional manifestation of it.

Man-made Elements

Atomic research has shown the way to create new elements by high-energy bombardment of the nuclei of existing elements. Adding or removing a neutron only produces a different isotope of the same element but whenever a proton is added or subtracted the element is changed. A particularly exciting search has been to add more protons and to produce elements with atomic numbers above 92. At the time of writing all elements up to 109 have been created and named. However, this is unlikely to be the end of the story and the search continues.

Whatever the positive charge in the nucleus, the same number of electrons are attracted and they settle into a new configuration with the lowest energy. So far, all the man-made elements have two electrons in the outer shell and they are therefore shown on the model on a single buttress.

Some of these new elements have half-lives measured in thousands or millions of years and will therefore continue to exist on Earth for a long time to come. However, as a general rule, as the atomic number increases, so the elements become increasingly unstable. Elements 108 and 109 have half-lives of only a few thousandths of a second and each of them has been detected essentially only by the manner in which it disappeared! It was a case of 'was here - rather than 'is here'! However, element 106 has an isotope with a half-life of over ten seconds and theory suggests that there may be other relatively stable elements in the range 112-118. According to theory, the most likely element for relative stability is 114 and it may well be identified in the next few years.

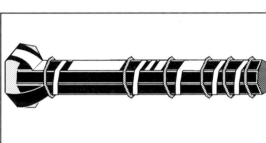

93	Neptunium	Np
94	Plutonium	Pu
95	Americium	Am
96	Curium	Cm
97	Berkelium	Bk
98	Californium	Cf
99	Einsteinium	Es
100	Fermium	Fm
101	Mendelevium	Md
102	Nobelium	No
103	Lawrencium	Lr
104	Rutherfordium	Rf
105	Dubnium	Db
106	Seaborgium	Sg
107	Bohrium	Bh
108	Hassium	Hs
109	Meitnerium	Mt
110	Ununnilium	Uun

Uranium is the heaviest element to exist naturally on Earth and is the final one on the main column of the model. All 92 elements have been discovered on Earth with just two exceptions, technetium and promethium. Neither has any stable isotopes and their other isotopes have half-lives which are too short for natural deposits still to exist. Technetium was the first example of an artificial element and it was first created in 1937 by adding a proton to the nucleus of molybdenum. Since its half-life is 4.2 million years, it will now be present on earth for a very long time into the future. The same cannot be said of promethium unless it is continually being remade because its most stable isotope has a half-life of only 17.8 years.

And Finally...

Many fundamental questions about chemistry and the elements have been answered and many problems solved but there are still many fundamental mysteries to resolve. In particular why electrons, protons and neutrons are as they are and how they relate to the other short-lived particles which nuclear physicists have discovered inside the atom.

If you have enjoyed this book then there may be other Tarquin books which will interest you. In particular,'The Curious Quantum' by Lee Bulbrook and 'DNA-The Marvellous Molecule' by Borin Van Loon. They are available from Bookshops, Toy Shops Art/Craft Shops or in case of difficulty directly from Tarquin Publications, Stradbroke, Diss, Norfolk IP21 5JP, England.

For an up-to-date catalogue, please write to Tarquin Publications, Stradbroke, Diss, Norfolk, IP21 5JP, England, or see us on the Internet at http://www.tarquin-books.demon.co.uk

The First Transition Metals

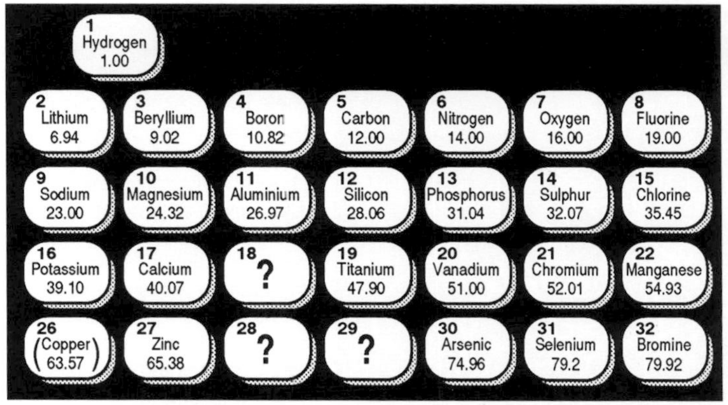

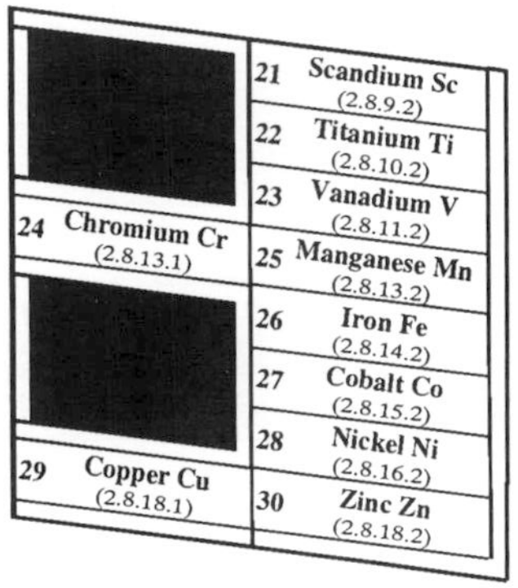

21 Scandium Sc (2.8.9.2)
22 Titanium Ti (2.8.10.2)
23 Vanadium V (2.8.11.2)
24 Chromium Cr (2.8.13.1)
25 Manganese Mn (2.8.13.2)
26 Iron Fe (2.8.14.2)
27 Cobalt Co (2.8.15.2)
28 Nickel Ni (2.8.16.2)
29 Copper Cu (2.8.18.1)
30 Zinc Zn (2.8.18.2)

The spiral nature of the chemical helix is broken for the first time by elements 21-30. There are exactly 10 of them as the five 3d orbitals fill. As might be expected, they all have many similar chemical properties because the filling is not taking place in the valence shell. However, they are clearly distinguishable and in the modern group numbering system they all belong to different groups. The colours on the model show a more traditional wider grouping corresponding to the division into the first, second and third transition metals.

The elements iron, cobalt and nickel are the first of what are known as the triads. They are the three elements which are strongly magnetic. All three are found together in meteorites. A surprising fact to notice about this section of the model is that Chromium and Copper do not remain in the 'two valence electron' column but both step back into the 'one valence electron' column. One would logically expect their electronic structures to be (2.8.12.2) and (2.8.17.2), and for the block of ten elements to be vertical on the model. However, the arrangements (2.8.13.1) and (2.8.18.1) have each slightly lower energy and so this is what actually happens in practice.

The Rare Earths

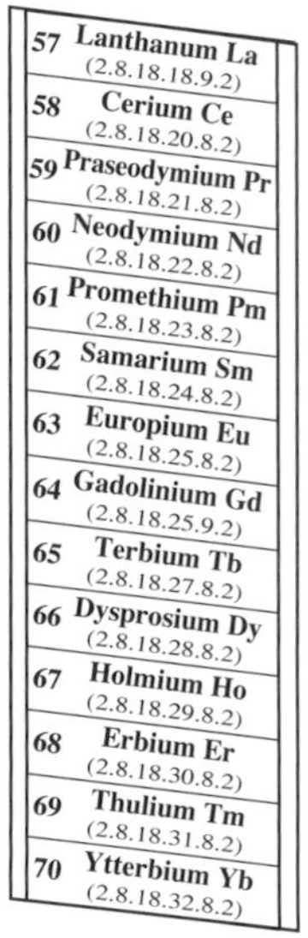

57 Lanthanum La (2.8.18.18.9.2)
58 Cerium Ce (2.8.18.20.8.2)
59 Praseodymium Pr (2.8.18.21.8.2)
60 Neodymium Nd (2.8.18.22.8.2)
61 Promethium Pm (2.8.18.23.8.2)
62 Samarium Sm (2.8.18.24.8.2)
63 Europium Eu (2.8.18.25.8.2)
64 Gadolinium Gd (2.8.18.25.9.2)
65 Terbium Tb (2.8.18.27.8.2)
66 Dysprosium Dy (2.8.18.28.8.2)
67 Holmium Ho (2.8.18.29.8.2)
68 Erbium Er (2.8.18.30.8.2)
69 Thulium Tm (2.8.18.31.8.2)
70 Ytterbium Yb (2.8.18.32.8.2)

The collective name of these fourteen elements is something of a confusion as they are neither rare nor earths. This misnaming arose because it was originally thought that their oxides were the elements. It was only later that their true nature was appreciated. All of them are soft, malleable metals and even the least common is as plentiful as iodine.

The most common element of the group, cerium, is more plentiful than either tin or lead but, unlike them, relatively few practical uses have been found so far. The best known is to make the 'flints' in lighters, as when combined with iron, it gives off a spark when struck. Some rare earths are ingredients in the exciting new discoveries of high temperature superconductors.

The rare earths are not widely spread around the globe, but are concentrated in a few particular sites in Scandinavia, Siberia, Greenland, North America, Brazil and India. The best known site is near Ytterby in Sweden, a place which has given its name to three elements, ytterbium, erbium and yttrium.

Notice how the outer shell of each of these elements contains 2 electrons and the next either 8 or 9 electrons. The filling of the seven 4f-orbitals takes place in the third shell from the outside and this explains why their chemical properties are so very similar to each other. Where one element occurs, so do most or all of the others and they are very difficult to separate. On the model they form a vertical column.

1 Hydrogen 1.00
2 Lithium 6.94
3 Beryllium 9.02
4 Boron 10.82
5 Carbon 12.00
6 Nitrogen 14.00
7 Oxygen 16.00
8 Fluorine 19.00
9 Sodium 23.00
10 Magnesium 24.32
11 Aluminium 26.97
12 Silicon 28.06
13 Phosphorus 31.04
14 Sulphur 32.07
15 Chlorine 35.45
16 Potassium 39.10
17 Calcium 40.07
18 ?
19 Titanium 47.90
20 Vanadium 51.00
21 Chromium 52.01
22 Manganese 54.93
26 Copper 63.57
27 Zinc 65.38
28 ?
29 ?
30 Arsenic 74.96
31 Selenium 79.2
32 Bromine 79.92

This diagram shows part of Mendeleev's periodic table in 1870, a year after he first proposed the idea. If you compare the order of the elements on the model with those here, you will see that although the order is substantially the same, the atomic numbers are different. However they are different in a systematic way.

Element	Mendeleev (1870)	Nowadays	Difference
Lithium	2	3	+ 1
Boron	4	5	+ 1
Sodium	9	11	+ 2
Chlorine	15	17	+ 2
Potassium	16	19	+ 3
Copper	26	29	+ 3

Any scientific theory is greatly strengthened if it can accommodate discoveries which are made after it is proposed and published. The idea of the existence of the periodic table received a great boost in 1875 when element 28, which Mendeleev called Eka-Aluminium, was discovered in a mineral from a mine in the Pyrenees. It is now called Gallium, after the ancient name for France, but it had all the properties that Mendeleev had forecast for it. Likewise, the discoveries in 1879 of Scandium to fill space 18 and of Germanium in 1886 to fill space 29 were exciting confirmations of the strength of the theory.

Even more remarkable was the discovery in the years up to the turn of the century of a whole unknown family of elements, the six inert gases: Helium, Neon, Argon, Krypton, Xenon and Radon. This was especially poignant as they are present in small quantities in all air and were therefore being breathed in with every breath by all the scientists looking for new elements! They are so chemically inactive that their presence had never even been suspected. This discovery added one new element to every row of the table and formed a complete new column. They also explain the differences of +1, +2, +3 in the table above.

Mendeleev's table then had eight columns and not seven. Nowadays it is no longer a mystery why there are eight and why the model has eight sides. Quantum mechanics is able to provide the answer and so this minibook is able to explain both 'The Anatomy of the Atom' and why the periodic table takes the form it does.

Mendeleev would have been delighted at the modern explanation and we hope that you too will find it a fascinating story.

A Simplified Anatomy of an Atom

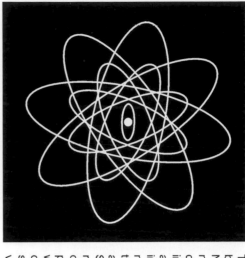

This model of the atom was proposed by Rutherford in 1919 and improved by Niels Bohr. Although it is now known not to be correct, it remains a convenient one to use as a mental image of what an atom is like. The anatomy of an atom divides naturally into two regions. Firstly there is a dense nucleus which occupies about one ten thousandth of the diameter of the atom and contains the protons and neutrons. Secondly there is a substantially empty region containing a whirling cloud of orbiting electrons. By far the greatest part of every atom is empty space. As we shall shortly see, atoms are considerably stranger than this diagram suggests. However, it does serve as a very useful starting point.

From the point of view of chemistry and the periodic table, it is sufficient to say that atoms are made up of three fundamental particles: protons, neutrons and electrons. Nuclear physicists know otherwise, but in considering the chemical properties of elements, particles such as mesons, positrons, neutrinos etc. can be safely ignored. Of the three particles we cannot ignore, protons have a positive charge, electrons have a negative charge and neutrons have no charge at all. It is a remarkable fact, so far unexplained, that the positive charge on the proton has precisely the same value as the negative charge on the electron.

How Big is an Atom?

Before we begin to consider the internal structure of atoms or find out what makes one element different from another, let us consider just how small an atom is.

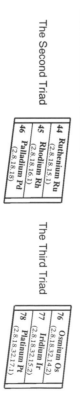

50mm — 500,000,000 atoms

1mm — 10,000,000 atoms

This printed line is 50mm long and 1mm wide. Black ink for printing is made by dispersing carbon in a solvent. When the solvent evaporates, the carbon atoms attach themselves to the molecules of the paper and the line can be seen. Roughly speaking there are 10,000,000 atoms per millimetre.

However, to print a line like this we are not thinking of a layer just one atom thick. In average printing, there has to be between 10,000 and 15,000 layers of atoms. If there were any fewer, the line or indeed these words you are reading, would look faded.

We can now calculate roughly how many carbon atoms are required just to make this line. There are at least

$$5 \times 10^8 \times 1 \times 10^7 \times 1 \times 10^4 = 5 \times 10^{19} = 50,000,000,000,000,000,000 \text{ atoms}$$

If you need convincing that atoms are very small indeed, then this calculation should do it!

Some Special Features of the Periodic Table

	Shell 1	Shell 2	Shell 3	Shell 4	Shell 5	Shell 6
29. Copper	2	8	18	1		
47. Silver	2	8	18	18	1	
79. Gold	2	8	18	32	18	1

	Shell 1	Shell 2	Shell 3	Shell 4	Shell 5	Shell 6
30. Zinc	2	8	18	2		
48. Cadmium	2	8	18	18	2	
80. Mercury	2	8	18	32	18	2

These two groups of three elements make up the 'third transition metals' and they are coloured an olive green on the model. They are found in the same relative positions above three of the shelves and share many chemical properties.

Although copper, silver and gold each have one valence electron and might be expected to be very active chemically, their inner shells have the magic numbers of 8, 18 & 32 and they go some way towards the stability of the inert gases. All three were known in antiquity and are sometimes found in their metallic form in nature. They have ores from which the metal can easily be extracted and have long been used for coinage. Since they are rather soft, they have to be alloyed with other metals to make them more wear-resistant. Copper with tin to make bronze, silver with copper to make sterling silver and gold with silver. They form a sub-group, now numbered 11 but previously numbered IB. If you look back to page 3 and the original table of Mendeleev you will see that copper was placed in the first column but was bracketed because he realised that it was not fully at home there. Now its position is understood.

Zinc, cadmium and mercury also form a sub-group (formerly IIB, now 12) and share many chemical properties. They are all resistant to atmospheric corrosion and are used in the manufacture of batteries of various kinds.

The Platinum Metals

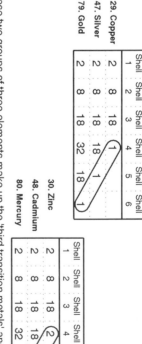

The Second Triad

| 44 Ruthenium Ru (2.8.18.15.1) |
| 45 Rhodium Rh (2.8.18.16.1) |
| 46 Palladium Pd (2.8.18.18) |

The Third Triad

| 76 Osmium Os (2.8.18.32.14.2) |
| 77 Iridium Ir (2.8.18.32.15.2) |
| 78 Platinum Pt (2.8.18.32.17.1) |

These two groups of three consecutive elements are coloured light green on the model. They are known as the light and heavy platinums and are all of similar appearance. All six metals have remarkable resistance to chemical attack, probably due to their lattice structure. They are found in nature in metallic form, often alloyed together.

Notice that palladium has no electron in its outer shell. It is the only element to break the valence electron rule and there should theoretically be no place for it on the model. One could say that it is the exception that proves the rule! Because its electronic structure might be expected to end with 17.1, that is where it has been placed on the model. However, 18 is such a magic number that the electron actually drops into the inner shell.

As an interesting fact, the standard metre in Paris, which originally served as a basis for the whole metric system of weights and measures is made of an alloy of platinum and iridium.

Protons, Neutrons and Electrons

Each element has a unique number of protons and this number is known as the atomic number. For every proton in the nucleus there is an electron in orbit around it and within all nuclei heavier than hydrogen, there are also a certain number of neutrons. The table below gives data for the first four elements of the periodic table.

Element	Hydrogen	Helium	Lithium	Beryllium
Atomic Number	1	2	3	4
Protons in the nucleus	1	2	3	4
Neutrons in the nucleus	0 or 1	2	3 or 4	5
Electrons in orbit	1	2	3	4

We must now consider the significance of the alternative numbers of neutrons in the nucleus.

What are Isotopes?

Although Silicon always has 14 protons or it would not be silicon, there are stable forms with either 14, 15 or 16 neutrons. These are known as 'isotopes of silicon'. They all behave identically chemically and a normal sample of silicon, as for instance when combined with oxygen (which also has three stable isotopes) in sand at the seaside, will contain all three types in fixed percentages. So when you next visit the beach, think 'isotopes'!

Isotope	Protons	Neutrons	Electrons	Abundance
Silicon 28	14	14	14	92.23%
Silicon 29	14	15	14	4.67%
Silicon 30	14	16	14	3.10%

All nuclei are a jumbling mass of protons and neutrons which both repel and attract each other and only certain combinations are stable enough to remain in existence for long. Both protons and neutrons are very strongly attracted to each other by what is known as the 'strong nuclear force', but protons are driven apart from each other because of their positive charges. This electrostatic force of repulsion acts over larger distances than the strong nuclear force.

For stability, the attraction must be greater than the repulsion and for lighter elements, the ratio of neutrons and protons which give stable isotopes, tends to be about one to one. As the atomic number increases, so does the ratio. For instance, the stable forms of lead (82 protons) have 124, 125 and 126 neutrons.

The Transmutation of Elements

For a proton to enter or escape from a nucleus demands an enormous amount of energy. Much more than any chemical reaction can supply. That is why elements seem so stable and why one never changes into another in a chemical reaction. The dream of the ancient alchemists of being able to change lead or mercury into gold by discovering some cunning mixture, process or potion is disappointingly impossible.

However, one element can change into another through a nuclear reaction and the first clear demonstration that it was possible was given by Rutherford in 1919. He changed Nitrogen (7 protons) into Oxygen (8 protons) by bombarding the nucleus with helium nuclei. Elements are also transmuted when the nuclei of radioactive elements spontaneously split into smaller parts and produce a whole range of lighter elements. However, this is nuclear physics rather than chemistry and we will not consider it further in this minibook.

Eight is a Magic Number

The model has 8 sides and those elements which have the same number of electrons in the valence shell come vertically above and beneath each other. Each face of the model therefore shows a distinct chemical group. The groups are most clearly defined when the s-orbitals and the p-orbitals are being filled and the chemical helix is fully established. When electrons are filling the d-orbitals and the f-orbitals and inner shells, the helix is broken and the elements step vertically downward. Sometimes they even step backwards in what seems a rather random fashion before the helix resumes.

The 'shelves' on the model indicate where a new shell starts, so all the elements on a section between two shelves have electrons in the same number of shells. Elements with many chemical properties in common are in the same position relative to successive shelves.

That there are from one to eight valence electrons explains why Mendeleev's cards had to be placed into eight columns (after the discovery of the inert gases). It also explains that any manifestation of the periodic table with some kind of eight-fold symmetry will bring the elements of the main chemical groups into some significant alignment. You will see such alignments in the 'Community of the Elements Mobile', the 'Spiral Periodic Table' and of course in any standard two-dimensional lay-out of the periodic table. 'The Family Group Card' shows the old group numbers and also the new ones which are proposed as a consequence of the latest understanding of the electronic structure of the atom.

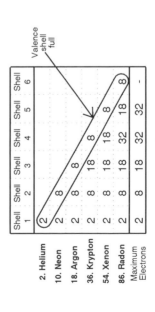

Complete Shells

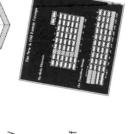

	Shell 1	Shell 2	Shell 3	Shell 4	Shell 5	Shell 6	
2. Helium	2						
10. Neon	2	8					
18. Argon	2	8	8				
36. Krypton	2	8	18	8			
54. Xenon	2	8	18	18	8		
86. Radon	2	8	18	32	18	8	← Valence shell full
Maximum Electrons	2	8	18	32	32	–	

As we have seen, a complete shell of electrons has a considerable stability and resistance to interference from other atoms. Once a shell is complete, it plays little role in chemical reactions. This point is strongly made when we consider those elements where all of their shells are full. Such elements, the inert gases, can scarcely be persuaded to take part in any chemical reactions at all and no compounds of Helium, Neon or Argon have yet been discovered.

How Heavy is an Atom?

The mass of an electron (9.1095×10^{-31} kg) is found to be only about one 1840th of the mass of a hydrogen atom. This means that virtually all its mass comes from the proton (1.6726×10^{-27} kg). A neutron (1.6750×10^{-27} kg) has similar mass to a proton and it is normal practice to ignore the electrons altogether in chemistry calculations. Useful working values for the masses of the component parts of the atom are given below. They can be used to calculate some interesting results.

Electron	Proton	Neutron
Zero	1.67×10^{-27} kg	1.67×10^{-27} kg

How Many Atoms or Molecules?

Using the values above we can calculate the mass of any atom or molecule and also find out how many there are in any given mass or volume. Here are three calculations to demonstrate how this works.

(a) What is the mass of a water molecule?
A water molecule is made up of 2 atoms of hydrogen and 1 of oxygen.
The nucleus of an oxygen atom contains 8 protons and 8 neutrons.
The nucleus of a hydrogen atom has 1 proton.
So the water molecule contains 18 particles each with a mass of 1.67×10^{-27} kg.
Therefore the mass is

$$18 \times 1.67 \times 10^{-27} \text{kg} = 3.006 \times 10^{-26} \text{kg}$$

(b) How many molecules are there in a litre of water?
A litre of pure water weighs 1kg and we now know the mass of a single molecule.
Therefore the number of molecules is $1 \div 3.006 \times 10^{-26}$, giving 3.33×10^{25}.

Writing this out in full, there are approximately
33,300,000,000,000,000,000,000,000 molecules

(c) How many atoms are there in a litre of hydrogen?
A litre of hydrogen at standard temperature and pressure weighs 0.00009kg.
So the number of atoms is obtained by dividing 0.00009 by 1.67×10^{-27}.
This gives approximately

The Mass Number

Interesting as it may be to perform calculations like the ones above, the masses of individual atoms are so small and the numbers so large that for most purposes it is best to work in a more convenient unit. One such unit is the 'mass number'. The mass number is the total number of neutrons and protons in an atom or molecule and we have in fact used it in calculation (a) above. The mass number of water is 18.

Different isotopes have different mass numbers and can be distinguished in that way. For example, the mass number of hydrogen can be either one (ordinary hydrogen) or two (deuterium). Deuterium has one proton and one neutron and is commonly known as 'heavy hydrogen'. About one atom in 6000 in naturally occurring hydrogen is heavy hydrogen and one of its uses is as a fuel in thermonuclear bombs. Deuterium combines with oxygen in just the same way as ordinary hydrogen to give not H_2O but D_2O (heavy water). This is used in nuclear reactors, not as a fuel but to slow down and moderate the reaction.

An unstable isotope of hydrogen called tritium also exists and it has a mass number of three.

Filling the Shells

This table shows the systematic way in which the orbitals fill up. Orbital 1s is the first to fill because it has the lowest energy of all. The single electron of hydrogen enters it and then the second electron of helium completes the electron-pair.

Element 3 is lithium with three electrons. Two fill orbital 1s and the third enters the orbital with the next lowest energy, namely 2s. With beryllium, orbital 2s is full.

The next electrons go into the 2p-orbitals and there are three of them. There will be no electron-pairs until all have a single electron in them. This situation is reached with nitrogen. Oxygen, fluorine and neon have respectively one, two and three electron-pairs and then the second shell is full.

So it continues, in a satisfying and logical way until the periodic table is complete.

Orbital	Max Electrons	Element	Electronic Structure
1s	2	1. Hydrogen	1
		2. Helium	2
2s	2	3. Lithium	2.1
		4. Beryllium	2.2
2p	6	5. Boron	2.3
		6. Carbon	2.4
		7. Nitrogen	2.5
		8. Oxygen	2.6
		9. Fluorine	2.7
		10. Neon	2.8
3s	2	11. Sodium	2.8.1
		12. Magnesium	2.8.2
3p	6	13. Aluminium	2.8.3
		14. Silicon	2.8.4
		15. Phosphorus	2.8.5
		16. Sulphur	2.8.6
		17. Chlorine	2.8.7
		18. Argon	2.8.8

A Reality Warning

The diagram opposite looks very clear and the 'Building up Principle' undoubtedly explains the structure of the periodic table brilliantly. However, do realise that the diagram gives the general idea, not the specific values for a particular element. The exact values of the energy levels within an atom depend both on the number of protons present in the nucleus and of course on the number of electrons in orbitals. Therefore the pattern for each element is unique. This point has been fully made when discussing the spectra, but it is important to keep it in mind.

Valence Electrons

If you look at the diagram opposite you will see that the 4s, 5s, 6s, & 7s-orbitals step downwards and are of lower energy than the d & f-orbitals of previous shells. This means that electrons will enter these s-orbitals and start a new shell before the previous shell or shells are full. It is also true that the p-orbitals of one shell always have lower energy than the s-orbitals of the next. A most important consequence which follows from this fact is that the outermost shell never contains more than 8 electrons.

When we talk about the chemical properties of an element, we are really talking about the way that it reacts and combines with other elements. These reactions are determined by electronic structures because when elements bond together to form compounds, they transfer or share electrons. The general name of 'valence' is given to the tendency to form compounds by a change in the electronic structure and so those electrons most involved in reactions with other atoms, those in the outer shell, are called the 'valence electrons'.

There can be either 1, 2, 3, 4, 5, 6, 7 or 8 valence electrons and no more and this is the underlying cause of the periodicity of elements which Mendeleev first observed. Elements which share the same number of valence electrons have many chemical properties in common. They form what is known as a 'chemical group' or a 'family group'.

The Relative Atomic Mass

The scientific community now uses a common standard for measuring the mass of atoms and molecules. They are given relative to Carbon 12 (mass number 12) which is taken to be exactly 12 units. This replaces the old standards based on hydrogen and oxygen. Samples of most naturally occurring elements contain mixtures of different isotopes and if the relative abundances are known, then the relative atomic mass can be calculated.

The three stable isotopes of silicon have mass numbers of 28, 29 & 30 and their relative abundances are given on page 5. The relative atomic mass is therefore

$$28 \times 0.9223 + 29 \times 0.0467 + 30 \times 0.031 = 28.1$$

This is an over-simplification but it shows how the calculation can be done. The published observed value for silicon is 28.0855.

The actual mass of an atom is always slightly less than the sum of the particles within it. This 'mass deficit' was explained by Einstein in terms of the energy which is released when forming the atom from its constituents through the famous relation $E = mc^2$.

Both Particles and Waves

Through all the discussion so far, it has been convenient to regard electrons, neutrons and protons as particles. However, quantum mechanics tells us that this is only one way of looking at them. They can also be described as waves. From the time of Newton there was a long debate about whether light was 'corpuscular' or particle-like or whether it was a kind of wave. The debate was finally settled when it was realised that it was both. A photon is a single particle of light and it also has a precise wavelength. One can imagine it as a packet of waves.

The French scientist, De Broglie showed how to calculate the wavelengths for particles of any size and proved that the greater the momentum (mass x velocity) of a particle, the shorter its wavelength. The shorter the wavelength, the more 'particle-like' it appears to be. We should therefore expect protons and neutrons to seem more like particles and electrons to seem more like waves. This is indeed how they behave and are generally regarded. However, we must never lose sight of the fact that all particles have this dual nature.

What is the Wavelength of Visible Light?

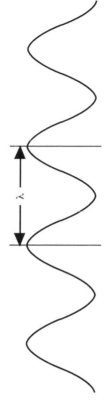

The wavelength of light is usually expressed by the Greek letter λ (lamda) where λ is the distance from the crest of one wave to the next. Nowadays it is usually expressed in nanometres (nm), where a nanometre is one thousand millionths of a metre (10^{-9} m). The wavelengths of light in the visible spectrum fall in the range of 650nm (red) to 400nm (violet).

Building up the Periodic Table

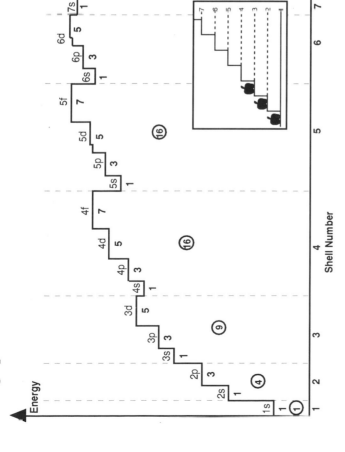

We introduced the idea of energy levels by means of seven ordinary steps and three apples. This diagram shows that the situation inside a many-electron atom is just a little more complicated. However, the basic idea is still the same.

Each horizontal step represents an energy level and at each level there can be either 1, 3, 5 or 7 orbitals. Since each orbital can hold a maximum of 2 electrons, individual steps can hold up to 2, 6, 10 or 14 electrons and not just a single apple! The seven original steps, numbered 1 to 7 represent the energy levels of the electron shells. However within all the shells except for the first, these are different energy levels associated with the orbital types of s, p, d & f. This means that the steps are divided into sub-steps. Some of them even step downwards.

It is this diagram, entirely predicted by quantum mechanics, which explains both the structure and the detail of the periodic table.

When the elements are placed in the order of their atomic numbers, then each element has one more proton and one more electron than the previous one. Let us imagine the extra electron being 'fed into' the system. It will naturally seek out the orbital with the lowest energy which is available to it. In this way the electronic structure of successive elements can be regarded as filling up from the inside as the atomic number increases. Since we know that each orbital can take a maximum of two electrons, the whole periodic table can be built up in a logical fashion one element at a time starting with hydrogen.

This process is known as the 'Building up Principle' or sometimes the 'Aufbau Principle' after the German word.

Quantum Jumps or Leaps

Electrons can only absorb or emit energy one quantum or very rarely two quanta at a time. They do this by jumping between different energy levels; up from a lower level to a higher one to absorb energy and down from a higher one to a lower to emit it.

This diagram shows some of the quantum jumps which are available within a particular atom. Each jump absorbs or emits a precise quantity of energy. The exact pattern of energy levels within a particular atom depends on the number of protons in the nucleus and is therefore unique to each element. So is the pattern of quantum jumps.

A common misunderstanding of quanta is to suppose that all quanta have the same amount of energy. They do not. The energy of a photon is proportional to its frequency and it is more convenient to express it in terms of frequency rather than wavelength.

Energy ▲

Level 7
Level 6
Level 5
Level 4
Level 3
Level 2
Level 1 (Ground State)

Frequency

The frequency of electromagnetic radiation, including visible light, is expressed by the Greek letter ν (nu). It is measured in Hertz (Hz) and is the number of waves which pass a fixed point in a second. The letter c is always used to represent the velocity of light.

Hence

$$\text{Wavelength} \times \text{Frequency} = \text{Velocity of light}$$

$$\lambda \quad \times \quad \nu \quad = \quad c$$

Using this formula, we can calculate the wavelength of light of any colour if we know the frequency and the frequency if we know the wavelength. The speed of light in a vacuum is 2.998×10^8 m/sec.

Example: What is the frequency of red light of wavelength 650nm?

The formula is used in the form $\nu = c \div \lambda$

Therefore the equivalent frequency is $2.998 \times 10^8 \div 650 \times 10^{-9} = 4.61 \times 10^{14}$

Hence a wavelength of 650nm is equivalent to a frequency of 4.61×10^{14} Hz.

The Energy of Photons

The energy of a photon is written as $E = h\nu$ where h is one of the fundamental constants of the universe, known as 'Planck's constant'. This constant is fundamental to quantum mechanics and has a very tiny value in m.k.s. units, which is why quantum mechanics is only important for microscopic happenings.

Energy per photon (10^{-24} J)

Lower Frequency		The Visible Spectrum	Higher Frequency	
Radio Waves	Infra-red	R O Y G B I V	Ultra-violet	X-rays
<0.1	20	28 32 34 37 42 45 47	60+	5000+

This table shows typical amounts of energy of photons of different frequencies in convenient units. It shows that a quantum of violet light (47 units) has nearly twice the energy of a quantum of red light (28 units). It also shows that a quantum of X-ray frequency contains more than 150 times more energy than a quantum of visible light.

The Spectrum

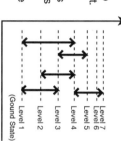

Red
Orange
Yellow
Green
Blue
Indigo
Violet

Most of us have seen what happens to sunlight when it passes through a prism. It was Isaac Newton in 1666 who first experimented in this way and who discovered that white light was in fact a mixture of colours.

In terms of photons we can say that white light is a mixture of photons of all colours and that a prism bends the paths of photons of different frequencies by different amounts. Red photons, those with the least energy, have their paths bent least and violet photons, those with the most energy, have their paths bent most. A prism is therefore able to sort photons by their frequency.

The Line Spectrum

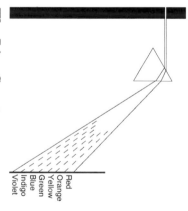

Since the pattern of energy levels and quantum leaps is unique to each element, each has a unique 'signature' of photon frequencies. These are emitted when the element is heated in a flame or excited by an electric current. If this emitted light is passed through a prism, each element produces a spectrum of coloured lines, a 'line spectrum' which is unique to that element. Each emitted frequency gives a distinct line in the spectrum.

This is the pattern of lines in the visible spectrum (The Balmer Series), which appears when hydrogen is burnt or excited and the light is passed through a prism. Confidence in the power of quantum mechanics as a scientific theory was greatly enhanced by the fact that the calculated wavelengths agree precisely with those observed by experiment.

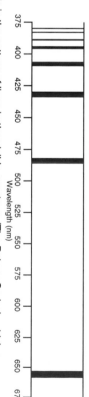

Wavelength (nm): 375 400 425 450 475 500 525 550 575 600 625 650 675

Spectroscopy

It was Bunsen and Kirschoff in 1859 who used the line spectrum as a method of identifying elements. As a method of analysis it had the great advantage that only minute quantities of the substance were required and that results could be obtained very quickly. This illustration shows the kind of instrument they used. The eyepiece allowed the spectrum to be magnified and the exact positions of the individual lines to be accurately determined.

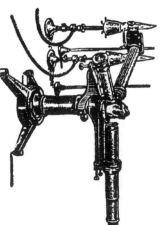

The first element they identified in this way was caesium. The name means sky-blue after the colour of the principle photons that it emits. This discovery was soon followed by that of rubidium. Its name was suggested by the dark red lines in its spectrum.

Instructions

1. Cut out the mobile roughly keeping well away from the final cut edge.
2. Then score carefully along the 6 short vertical score lines (as shown in the diagram). before cutting along the cut lines.
3. Fold as shown in the photo inside the front cover before hanging your finished mobile up by a thread sewn through the title piece.

Cutting & Scoring Plan

cut lines
fold lines

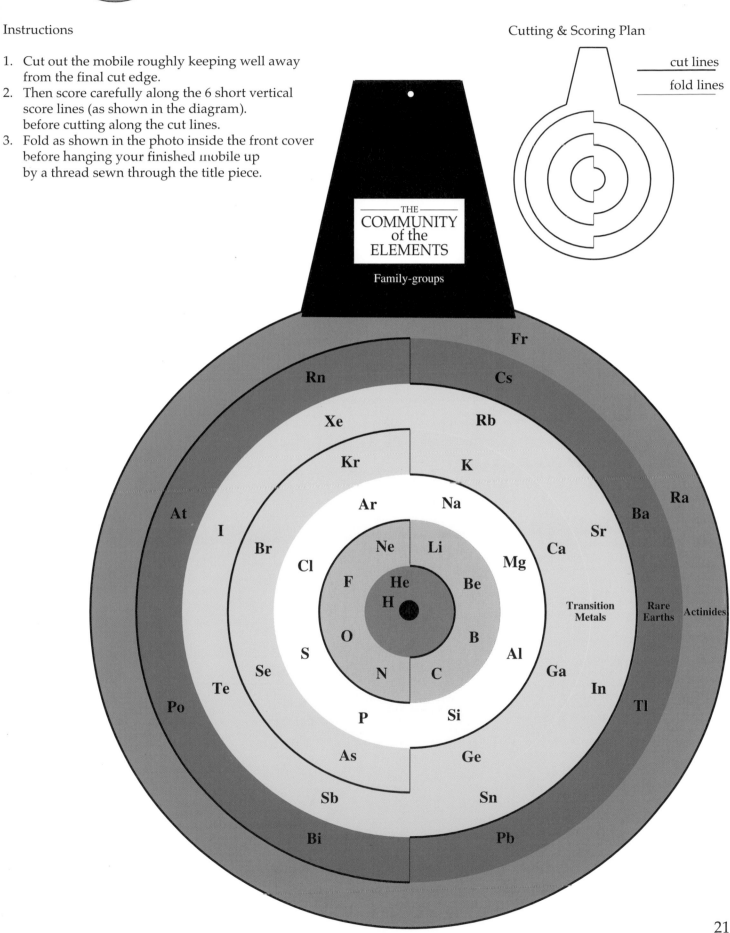

THE
COMMUNITY
of the
ELEMENTS

Family-groups

Fr

Rn

Cs

Xe

Rb

Kr

K

Ar

Na

Ra

Ba

At

Sr

I

Ne

Li

Ca

Br

Cl

Mg

F

He

Be

H

Transition
Metals

Rare
Earths

Actinides

O

B

S

Al

Se

N

C

Ga

Te

P

Si

In

Po

Ge

Tl

As

Sb

Sn

Pb

Bi

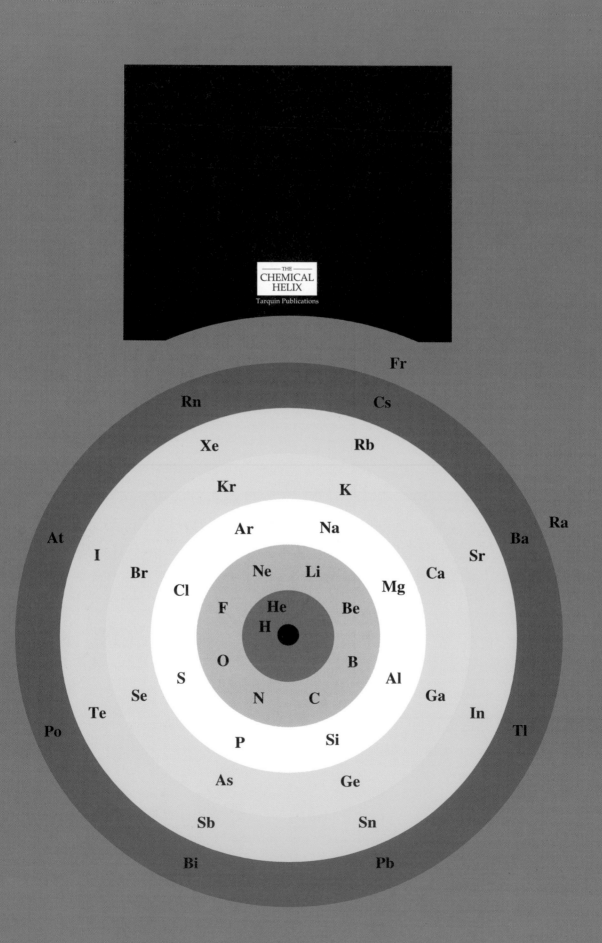

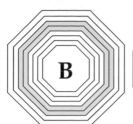
The 6 pieces for Module B are on this page and pages 7 & 9.

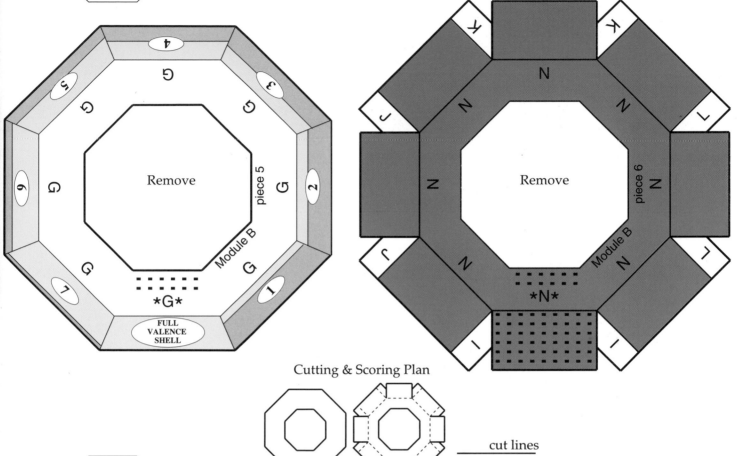

Remove

Module B

piece 5

G

G

FULL VALENCE SHELL

Remove

Module B

piece 6

N

Cutting & Scoring Plan

cut lines

fold lines

The 5 pieces for Module C are on this page and pages 25 & 27.

Cutting & Scoring Plan

cut lines

fold lines

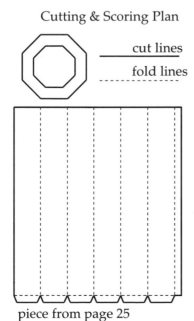

piece from page 25

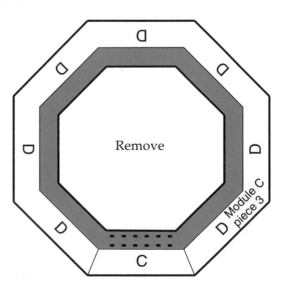

Remove

Module C

piece 3

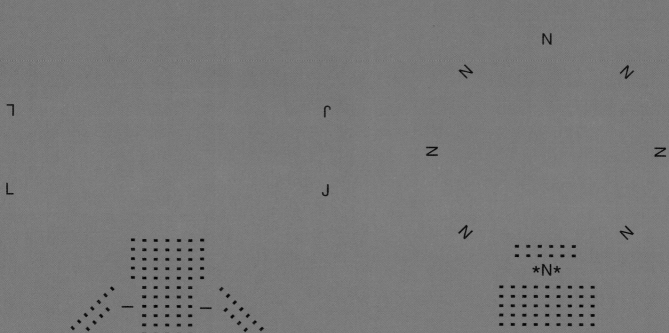

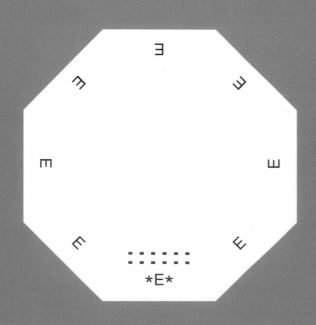

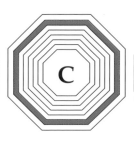

Elements 55 - 86

The 5 pieces for Module C are on this page and pages 23 & 27.

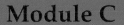

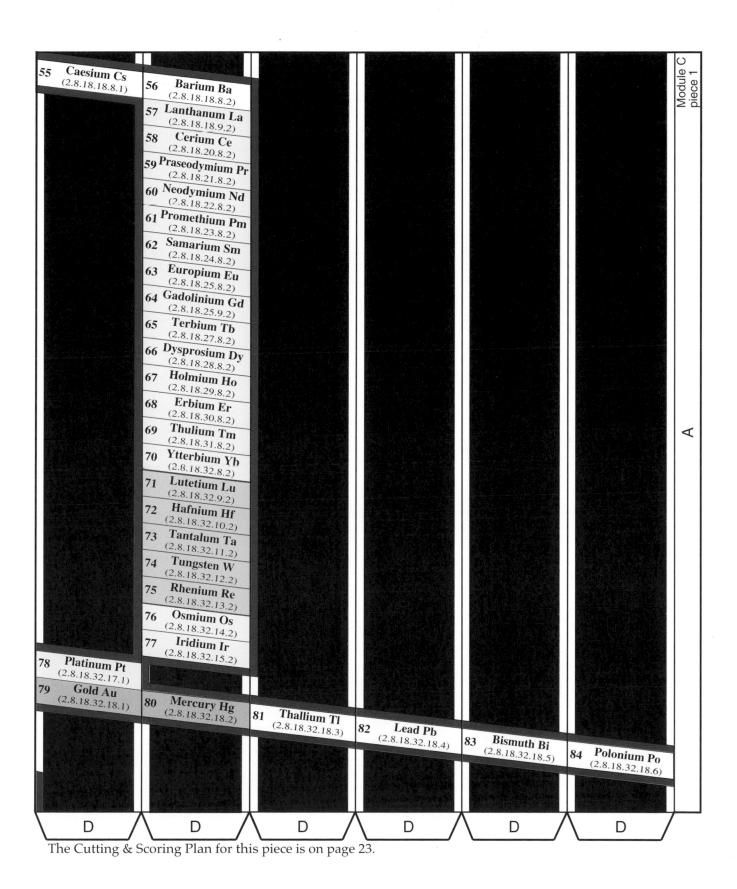

55	Caesium Cs (2.8.18.18.8.1)
56	Barium Ba (2.8.18.18.8.2)
57	Lanthanum La (2.8.18.18.9.2)
58	Cerium Ce (2.8.18.20.8.2)
59	Praseodymium Pr (2.8.18.21.8.2)
60	Neodymium Nd (2.8.18.22.8.2)
61	Promethium Pm (2.8.18.23.8.2)
62	Samarium Sm (2.8.18.24.8.2)
63	Europium Eu (2.8.18.25.8.2)
64	Gadolinium Gd (2.8.18.25.9.2)
65	Terbium Tb (2.8.18.27.8.2)
66	Dysprosium Dy (2.8.18.28.8.2)
67	Holmium Ho (2.8.18.29.8.2)
68	Erbium Er (2.8.18.30.8.2)
69	Thulium Tm (2.8.18.31.8.2)
70	Ytterbium Yb (2.8.18.32.8.2)
71	Lutetium Lu (2.8.18.32.9.2)
72	Hafnium Hf (2.8.18.32.10.2)
73	Tantalum Ta (2.8.18.32.11.2)
74	Tungsten W (2.8.18.32.12.2)
75	Rhenium Re (2.8.18.32.13.2)
76	Osmium Os (2.8.18.32.14.2)
77	Iridium Ir (2.8.18.32.15.2)
78	Platinum Pt (2.8.18.32.17.1)
79	Gold Au (2.8.18.32.18.1)
80	Mercury Hg (2.8.18.32.18.2)
81	Thallium Tl (2.8.18.32.18.3)
82	Lead Pb (2.8.18.32.18.4)
83	Bismuth Bi (2.8.18.32.18.5)
84	Polonium Po (2.8.18.32.18.6)

Module C
piece 1

A

D   D   D   D   D   D   D

The Cutting & Scoring Plan for this piece is on page 23.

B

C

Elements 55 - 86

Module C

The 5 pieces for Module C are on this page and pages 23 & 25.

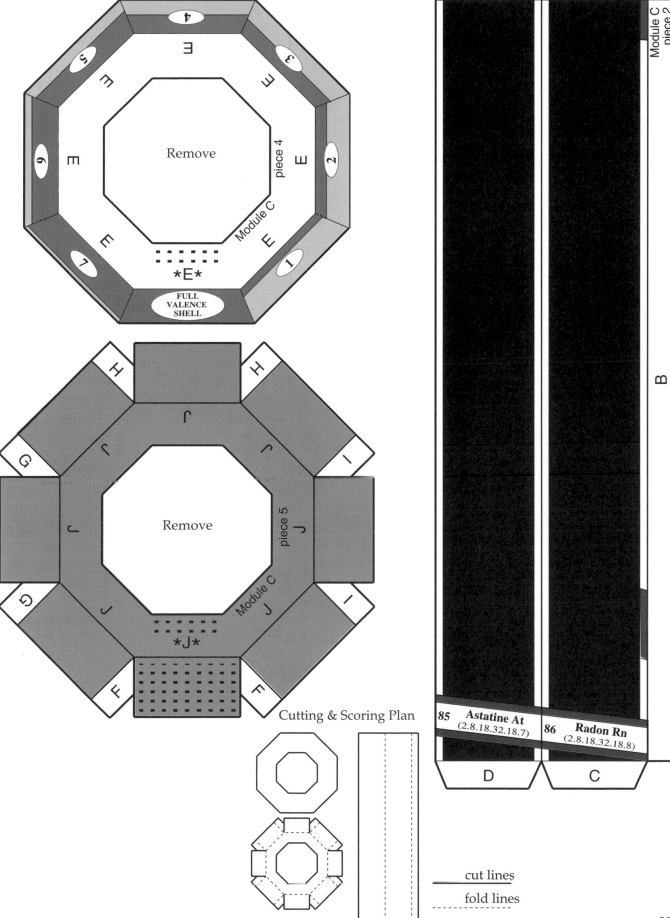

Remove

Module C
piece 4

E

FULL
VALENCE
SHELL

Remove

Module C
piece 5

J

Cutting & Scoring Plan

| 85 | Astatine At (2.8.18.32.18.7) |
| 86 | Radon Rn (2.8.18.32.18.8) |

Module C
piece 2

cut lines

fold lines

27

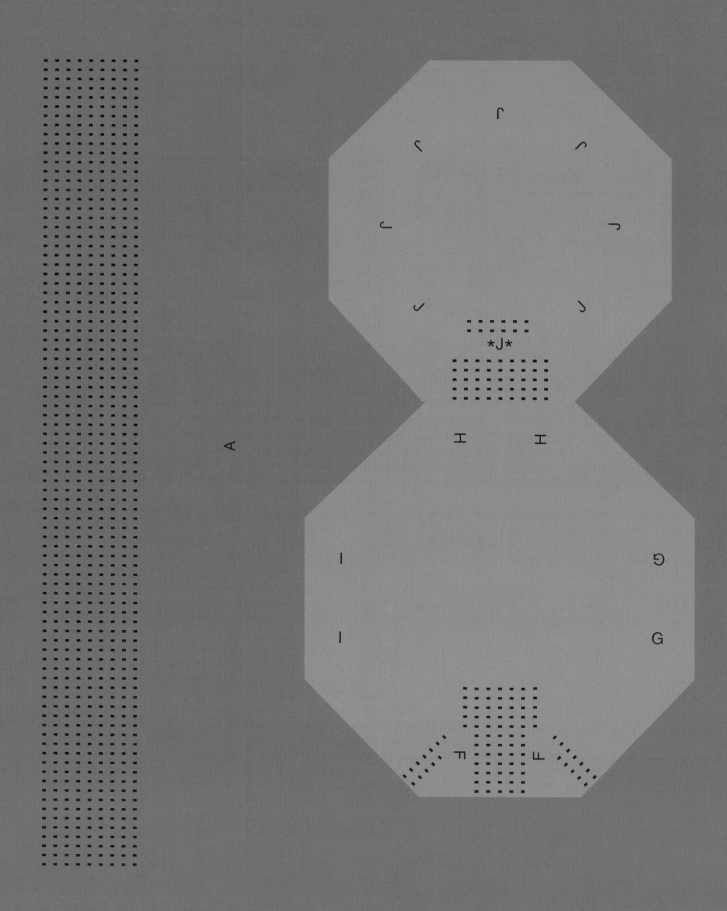

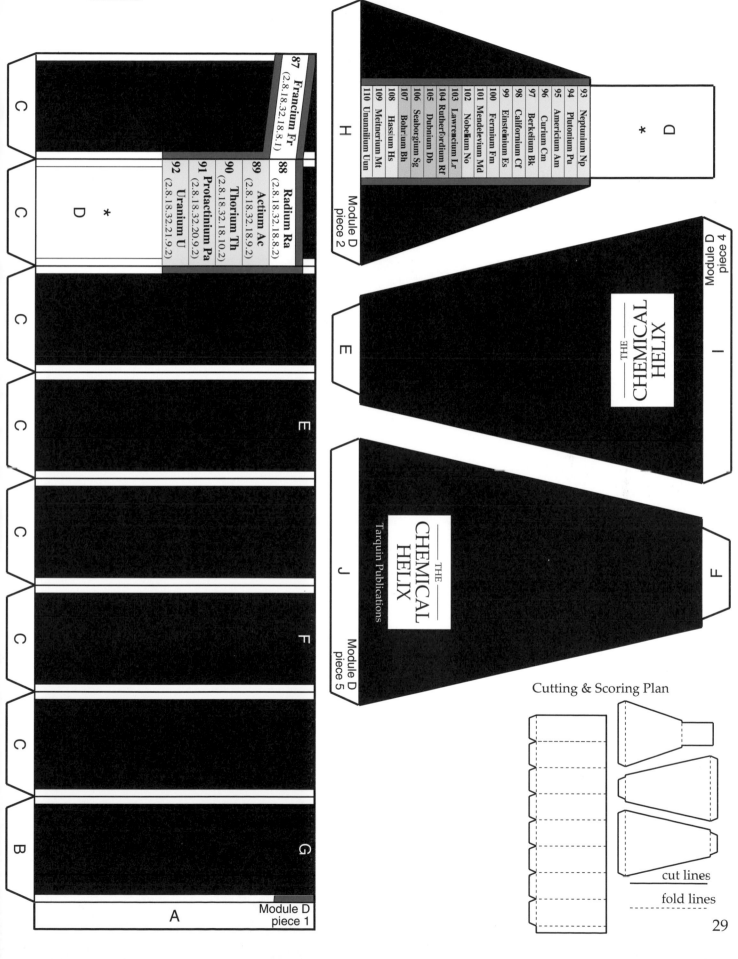

A

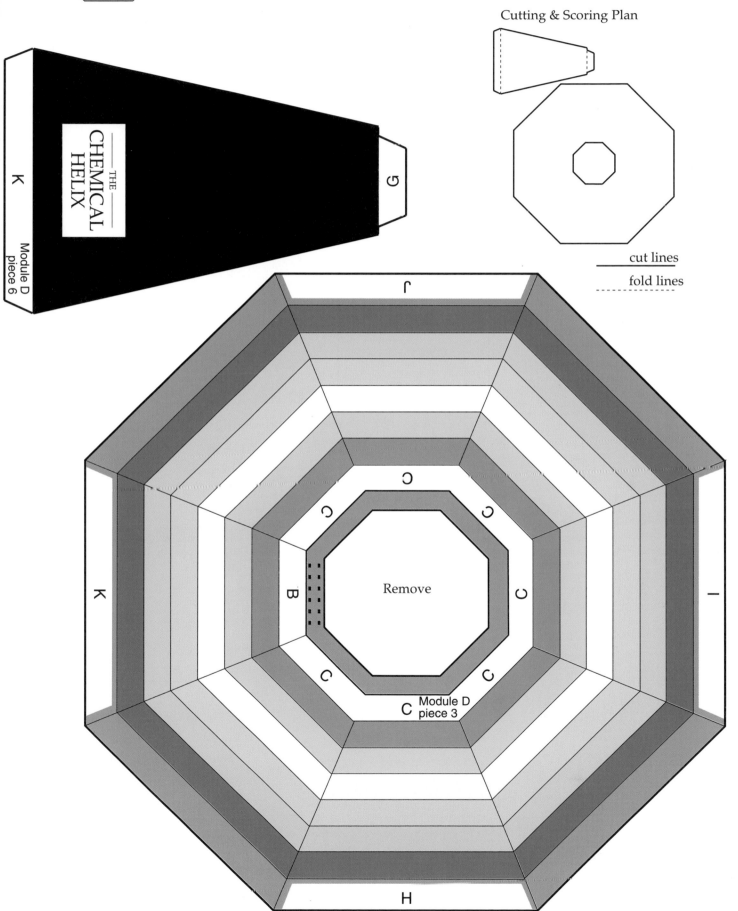

Cutting & Scoring Plan

cut lines

fold lines

THE
CHEMICAL
HELIX

K

G

Module D
piece 6

Remove

Module D
piece 3

C

B

K

I

J

H

C